Snarf

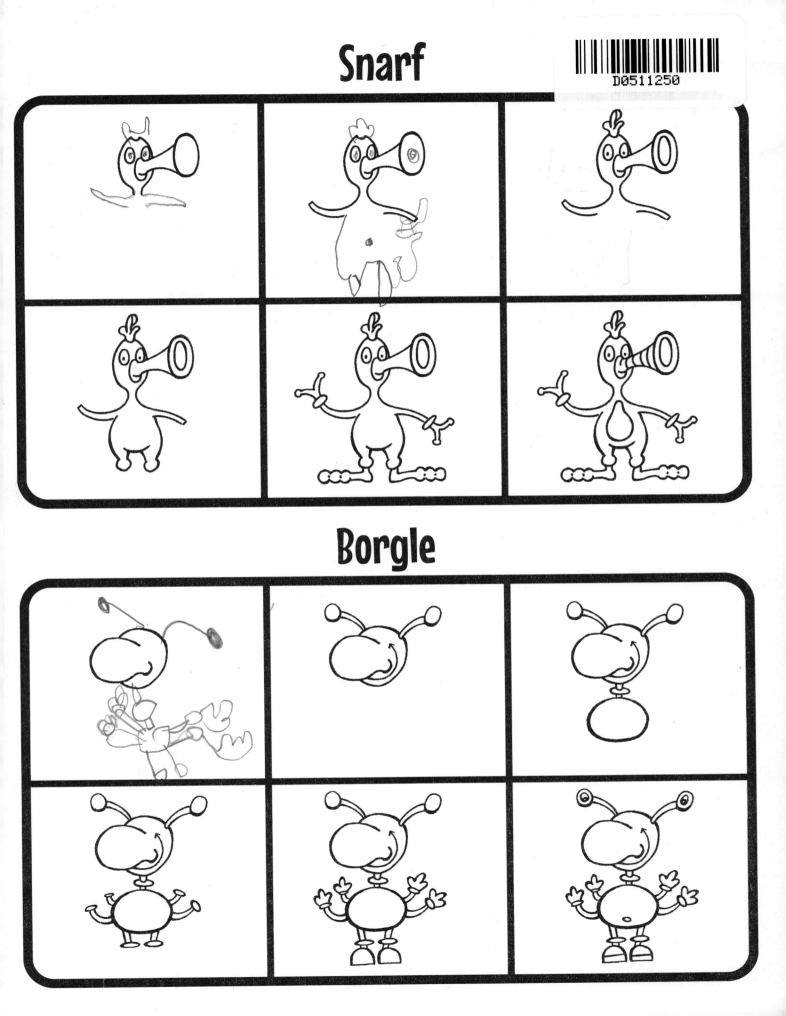

Borgle

Clopsy

Mutant

Marsian

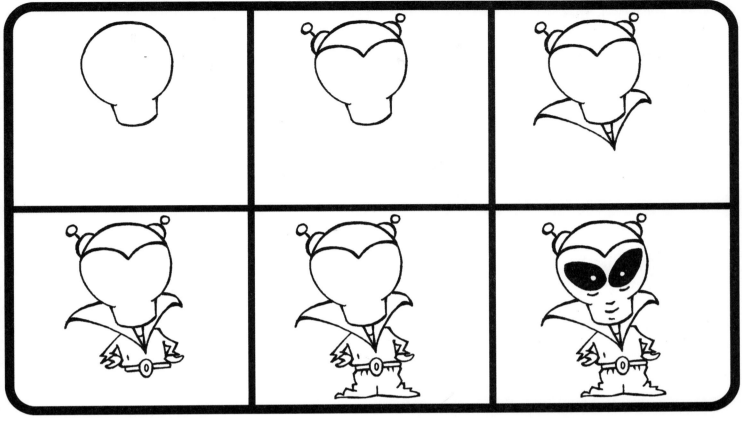

Starship Trooper

Amoeboid

Rocket

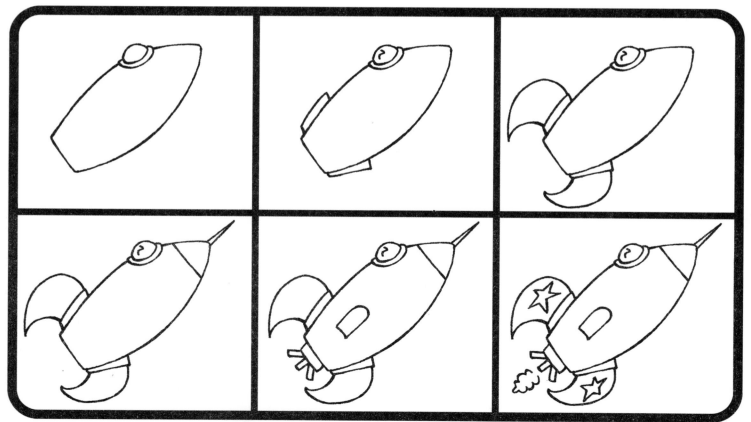

Predator

Flying Saucer

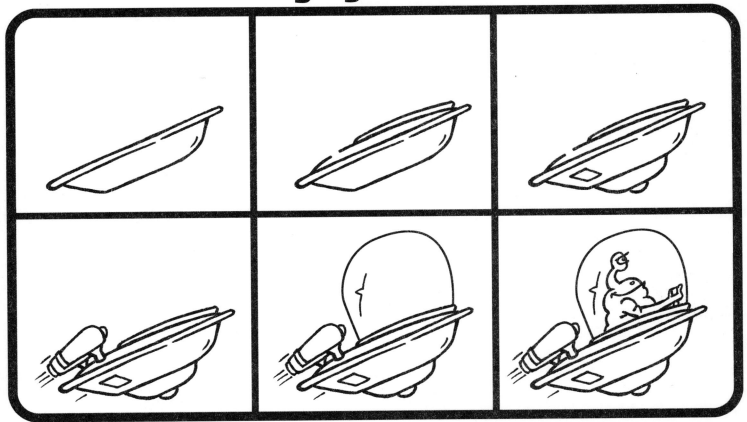

Delta

Zakbar

Big Banger

Gobble

Zoom

Battle Droid

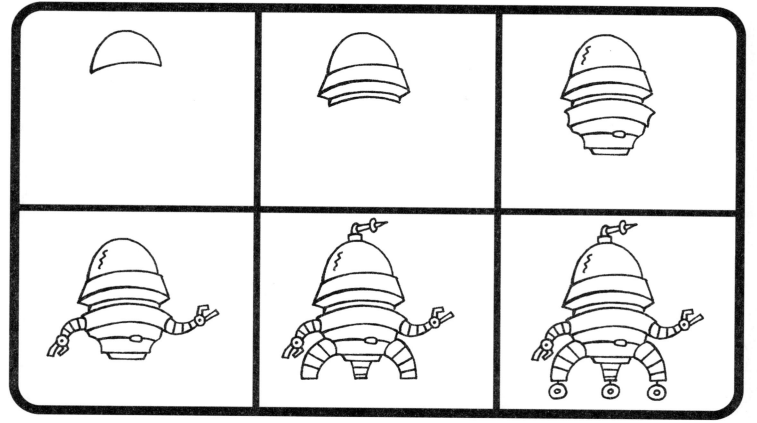

Asteroidus

Jabber

Lightspeed

Neutreno

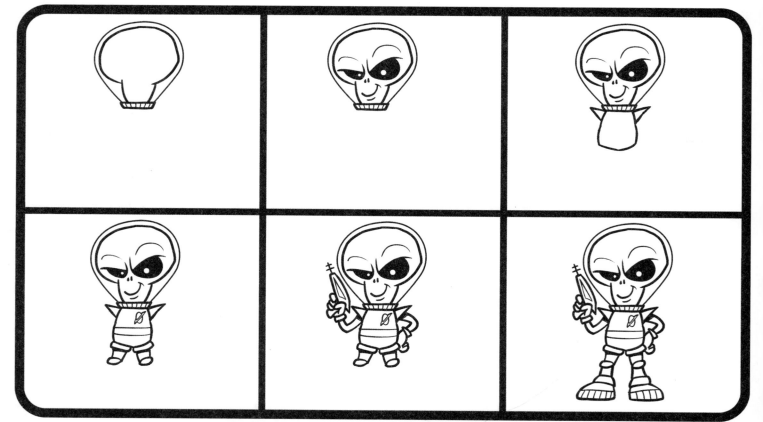

Laser

Worker Droid

Space Monkey

Fisheye

Spaced Out

Impact

Meteorus

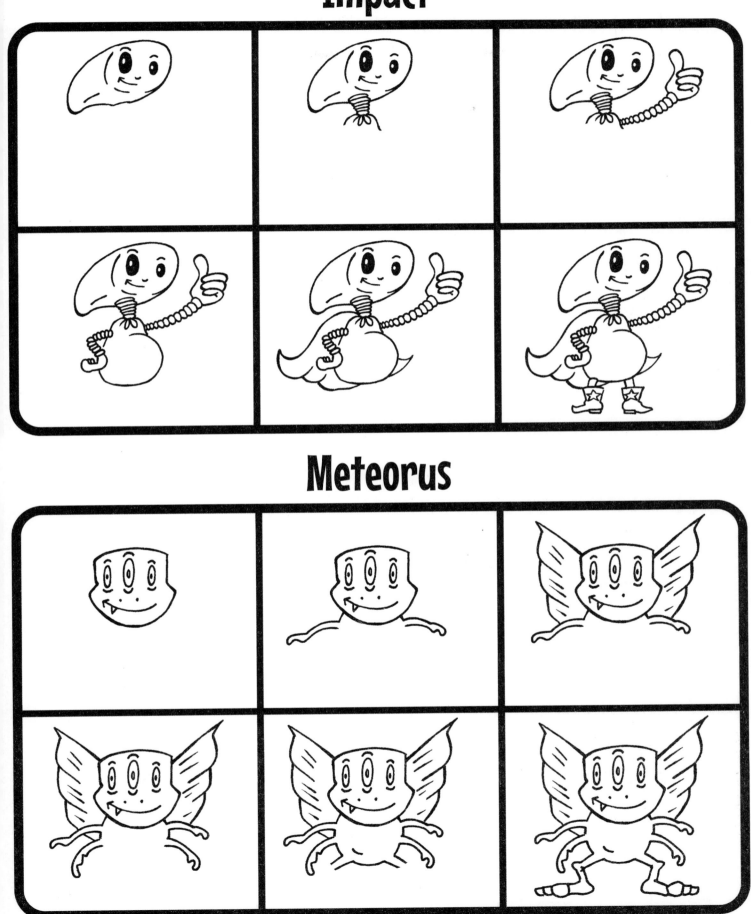

Lunar

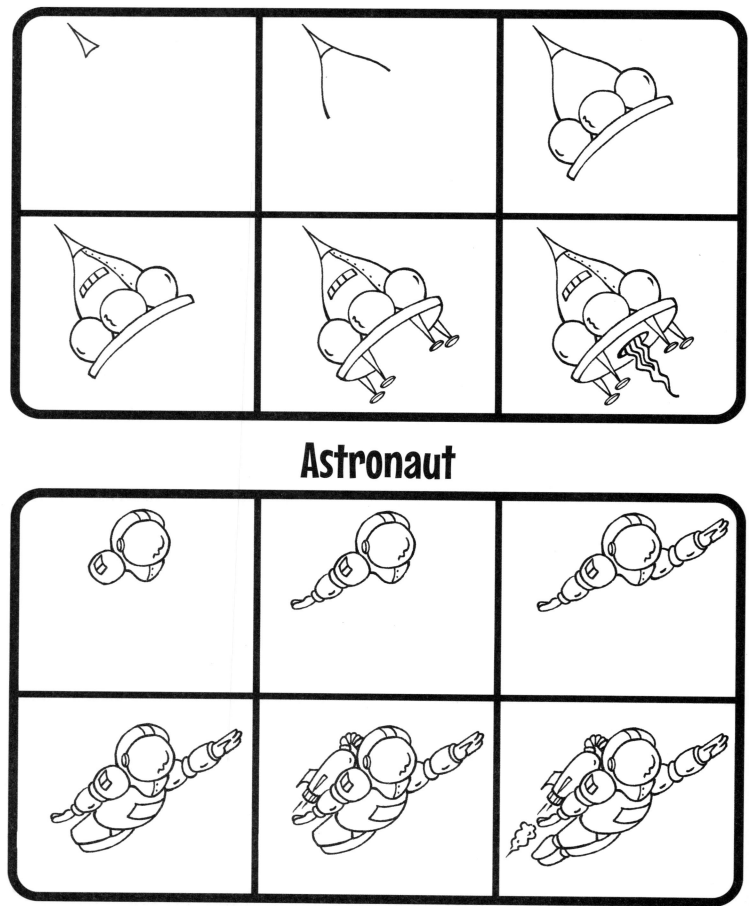

Astronaut

Elkan

Pluton

Alien X

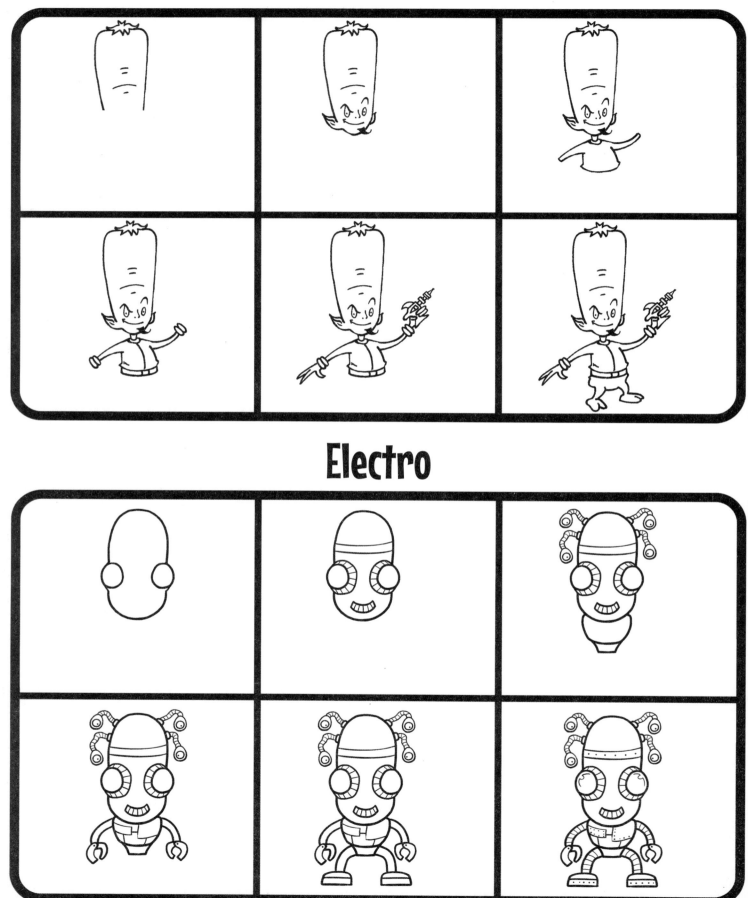

Electro

Nebulus

Starship Destroyer

Space Pirate

Gravitoid

Warp

Space Dog

Bugle

Apocalypse

Mollusc

Arachnid

Beagle

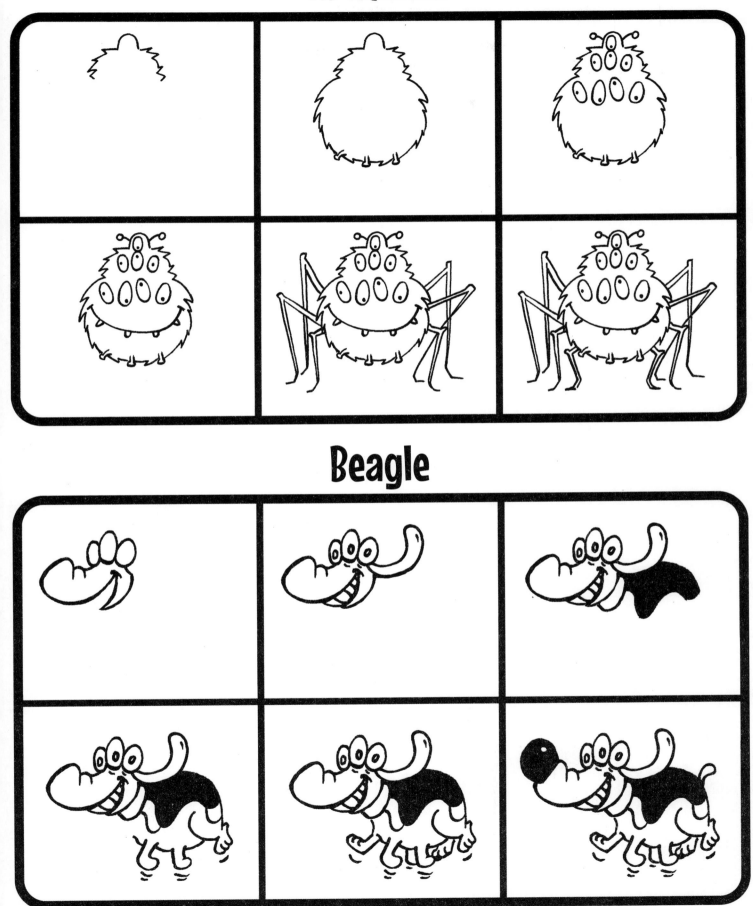

Blaster

Bounty Hunter

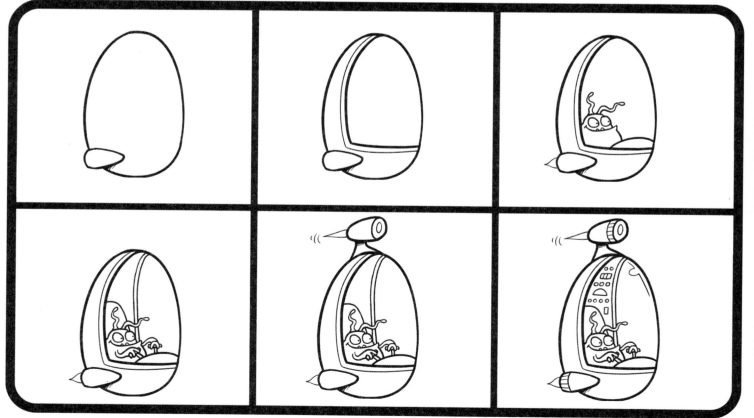

Zap

Starcrawler

Rocket Witch

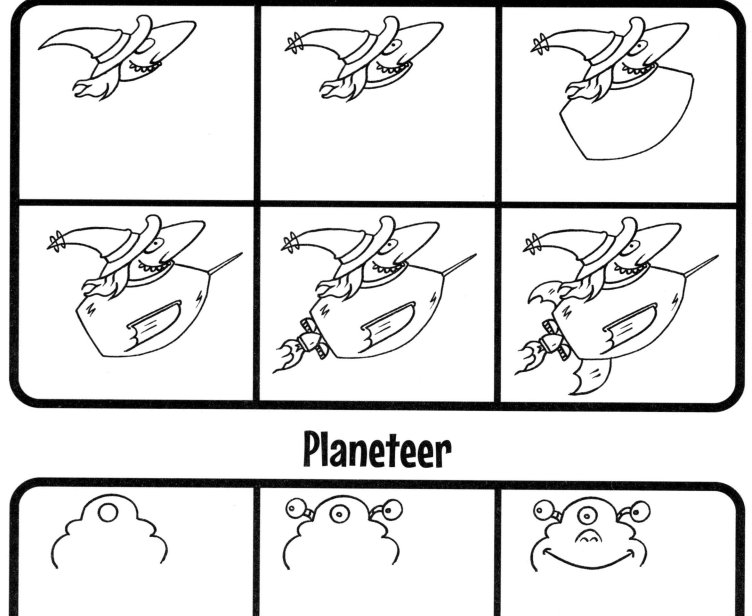

Planeteer

Moondusa

Moonpig

Matrix

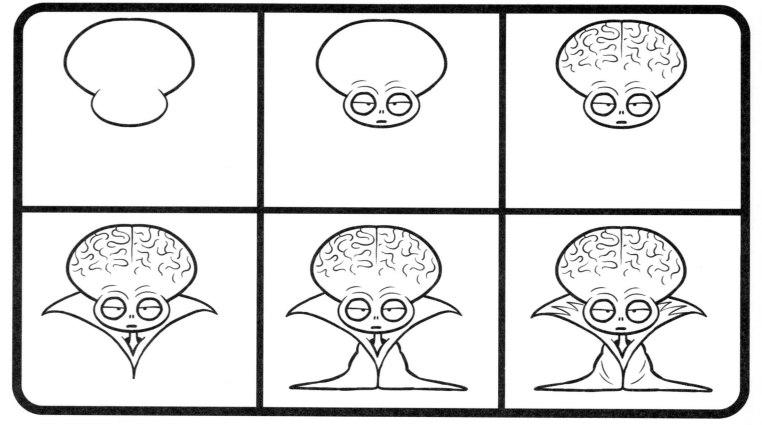

Infantry Droid

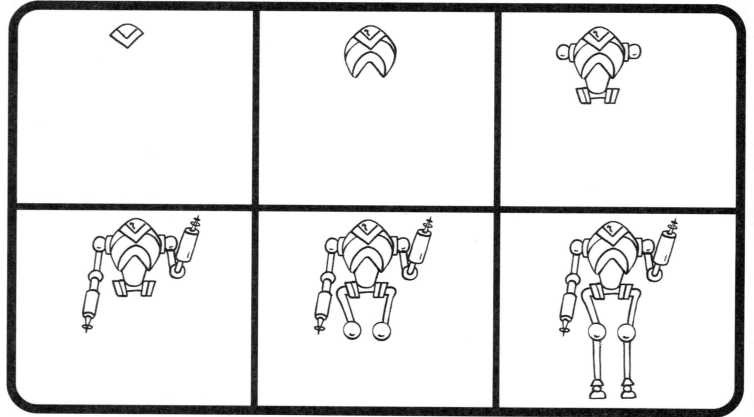

Nemotoad

Ice Planet Trooper

Star Man

Plasma

Space Troll

Dogworm

Thor

Crater Face

Saturn Hydra

Solar Windsurfer

Alien Pet

Vampoid

Space Rock Monster

Alien Medic

Space Raider

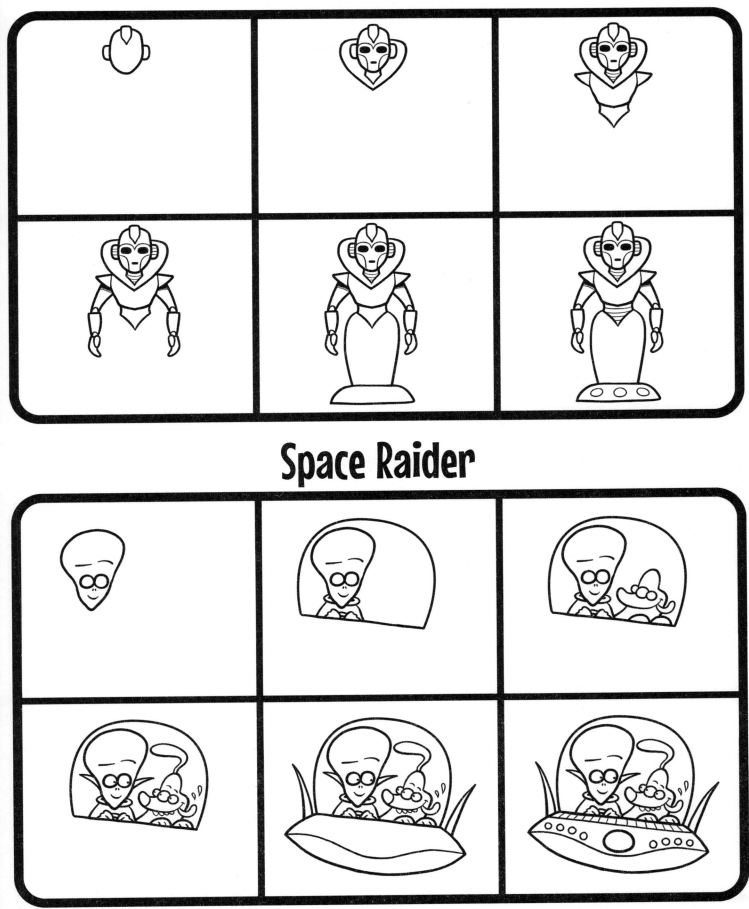

King of the Universe

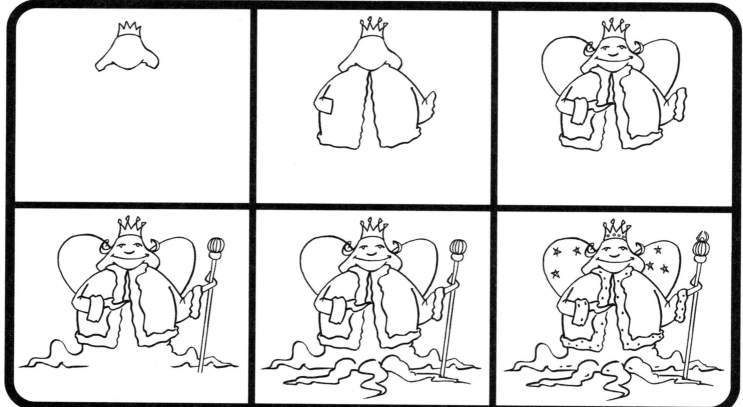

Queen of the Universe

Teleporter

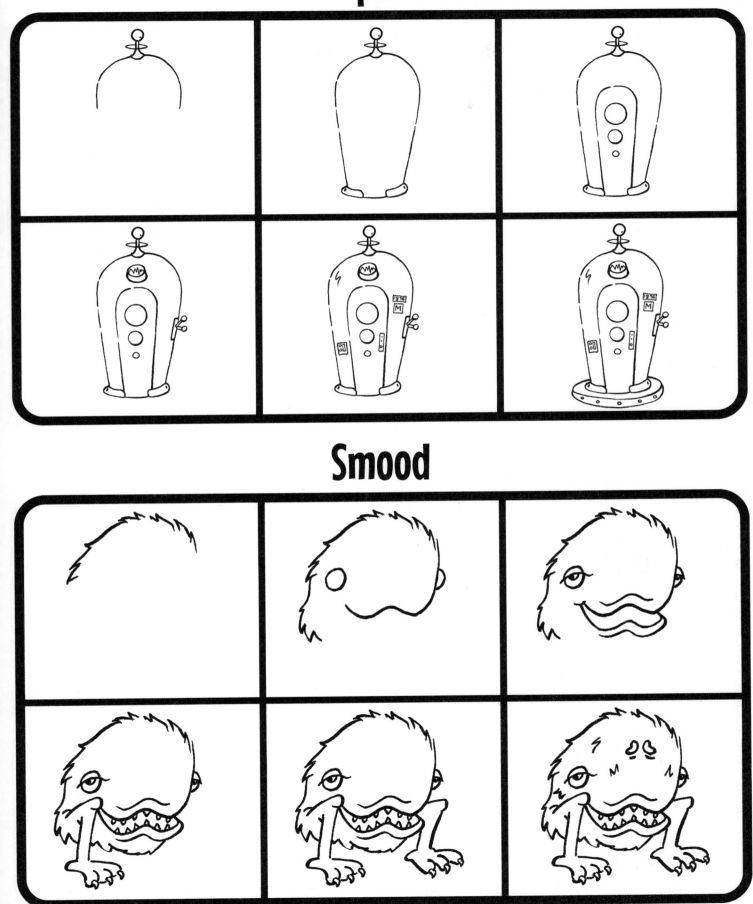

Smood

Vulcano

Kaboom

Ray Gun

Astral

Time Lord

Orbit

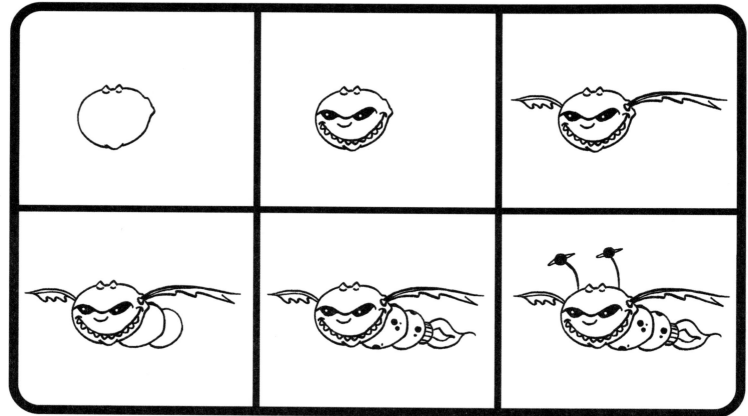

Helix

Atomic Kitten

Destroyer

Space Patrol Boat

Atmosfear

Daft Vader

Mugglepuff

Darth Mauler

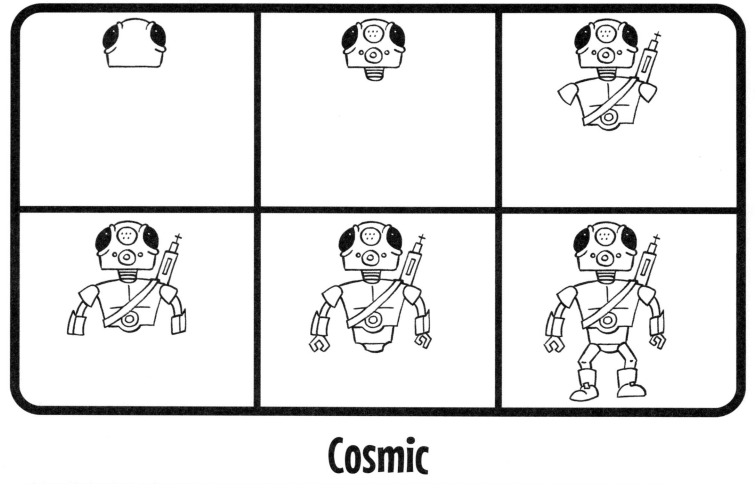

Cosmic

Solar Surfer

Obi-Wan Tinobi

Optimus

Neptunus

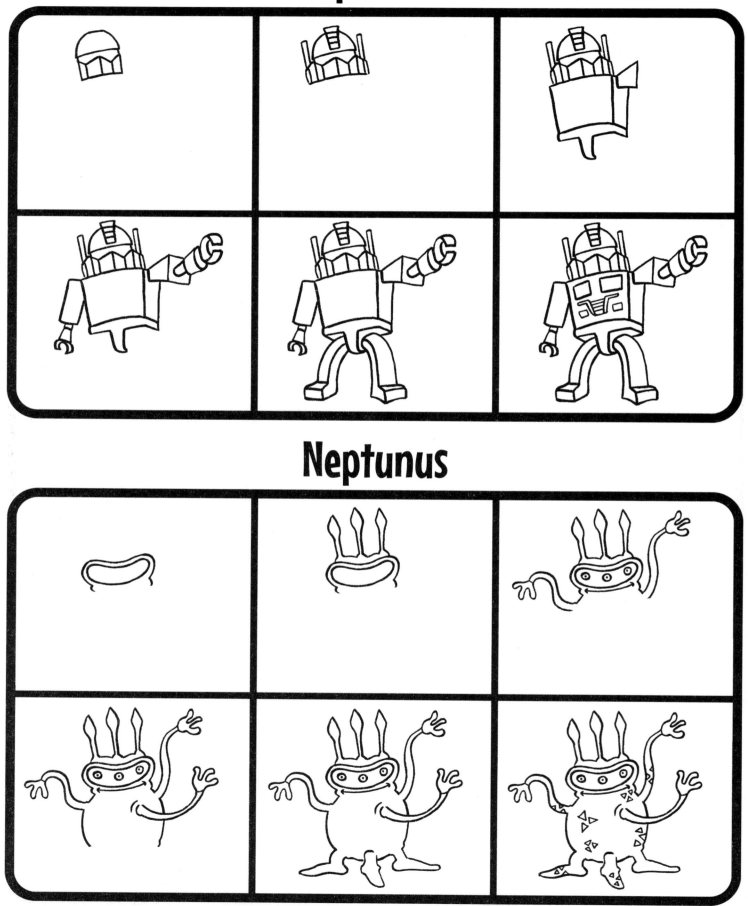

Space Sumo

Red Planet Beast

Fraggle

Dark Matter

Minx the Merciless

Alien Invader

Space Ghost

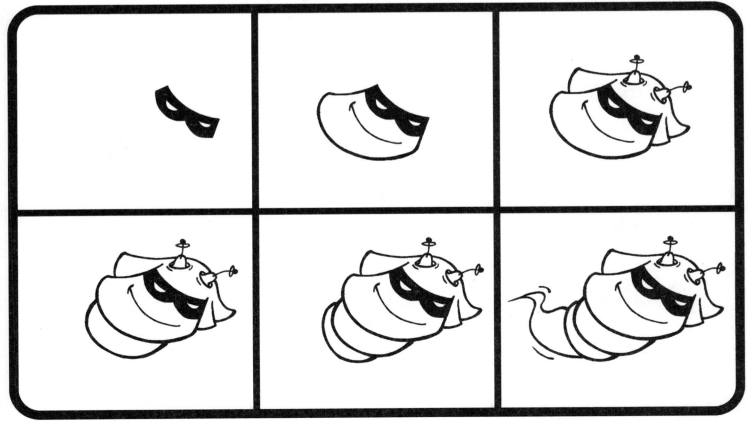

Star Warrior

Fission